HELLO beautiful

THIS SMART FITNESS PLANNER BELONGS TO:

....

SMART goals

SMART IS CONSIDERED THE BEST PRACTICE FOR SETTING GOALS. A SMART GOAL IS SPECIFIC, MEASUREABLE, ACHIEVABLE, REALIISTIC AND TIMELY.

SO, HOW DO YOU USE SMART TO ACHIEVE YOUR WEIGHT LOSS AND FITNESS GOALS?

S	YOUR WEIGHT LOSS AND/OR FITNESS GOALS SHOULD BE SPECIFIC.
M	YOUR GOAL SHOULD BE MEASURABLE. HOW WILL YOU MEASURE YOUR SUCCESS?
A	CREATE GOALS THAT ARE ACHIEVABLE. THINK ABOUT YOUR CURRENT SITUATION. MAKE SURE YOUR GOAL ISN'T OVERARCHING.
R	GOALS SHOULD ALSO BE REALISTIC. REMEMBER THIS ISN'T A SPRINT TO THE FINISH LINE.
T	GOALS SHOULD BE TIMELY. SETTING A TIME FRAME TO REACH YOUR GOALS WILL HELP TO KEEP YOU ACCOUNTABLE.

GOAL keeper

OVERALL GOAL	START DATE	REACH BY:

WHY IS THIS GOAL IMPORTANT?	REWARD
....	
....	
....	POTENTIAL OBSTACLES
....	

(BEFORE PICTURE)		
	ARM (R)	
	ARM (L)	
	CHEST	
	WAIST	
	HIPS	
	THIGH(R)	
	THIGH(L)	
	WEIGHT	
	BODY FAT	

FINAL RESULTS

(AFTER PICTURE)		
	ARM (R)	
	ARM (L)	
	CHEST	
	WAIST	
	HIPS	
	THIGH(R)	
	THIGH(L)	
	WEIGHT	
	BODY FAT	

MEASUREMENTS *tracker*

MONTH ONE	
WEIGHT	
+ / -	
ARM (R)	
+ / -	
ARM (L)	
+ / -	
CHEST	
+ / -	
WAIST	
+ / -	
THIGH (R)	
+ / -	
THIGH (L)	
+ / -	
BODY FAT	
+ / -	
TOTALS	
WEIGHT (+/-)	
INCHES (+/-)	
OTHER	

MONTH TWO	
WEIGHT	
+ / -	
ARM (R)	
+ / -	
ARM (L)	
+ / -	
CHEST	
+ / -	
WAIST	
+ / -	
THIGH (R)	
+ / -	
THIGH (L)	
+ / -	
BODY FAT	
+ / -	
TOTALS	
WEIGHT (+/-)	
INCHES (+/-)	
OTHER	

MONTH THREE	
WEIGHT	
+ / -	
ARM (R)	
+ / -	
ARM (L)	
+ / -	
CHEST	
+ / -	
WAIST	
+ / -	
THIGH (R)	
+ / -	
THIGH (L)	
+ / -	
BODY FAT	
+ / -	
TOTALS	
WEIGHT (+/-)	
INCHES (+/-)	
OTHER	

MONTH FOUR	
WEIGHT	
+ / -	
ARM (R)	
+ / -	
ARM (L)	
+ / -	
CHEST	
+ / -	
WAIST	
+ / -	
THIGH (R)	
+ / -	
THIGH (L)	
+ / -	
BODY FAT	
+ / -	
TOTALS	
WEIGHT (+/-)	
INCHES (+/-)	
OTHER	

MONTH FIVE	
WEIGHT	
+ / -	
ARM (R)	
+ / -	
ARM (L)	
+ / -	
CHEST	
+ / -	
WAIST	
+ / -	
THIGH (R)	
+ / -	
THIGH (L)	
+ / -	
BODY FAT	
+ / -	
TOTALS	
WEIGHT (+/-)	
INCHES (+/-)	
OTHER	

MONTH SIX	
WEIGHT	
+ / -	
ARM (R)	
+ / -	
ARM (L)	
+ / -	
CHEST	
+ / -	
WAIST	
+ / -	
THIGH (R)	
+ / -	
THIGH (L)	
+ / -	
BODY FAT	
+ / -	
TOTALS	
WEIGHT (+/-)	
INCHES (+/-)	
OTHER	

TODAY
IS YOUR DAY!
~ your ~
MOUNTAIN
IS WAITING.
so....
GET ON
YOUR WAY!

— DR. SEUSS

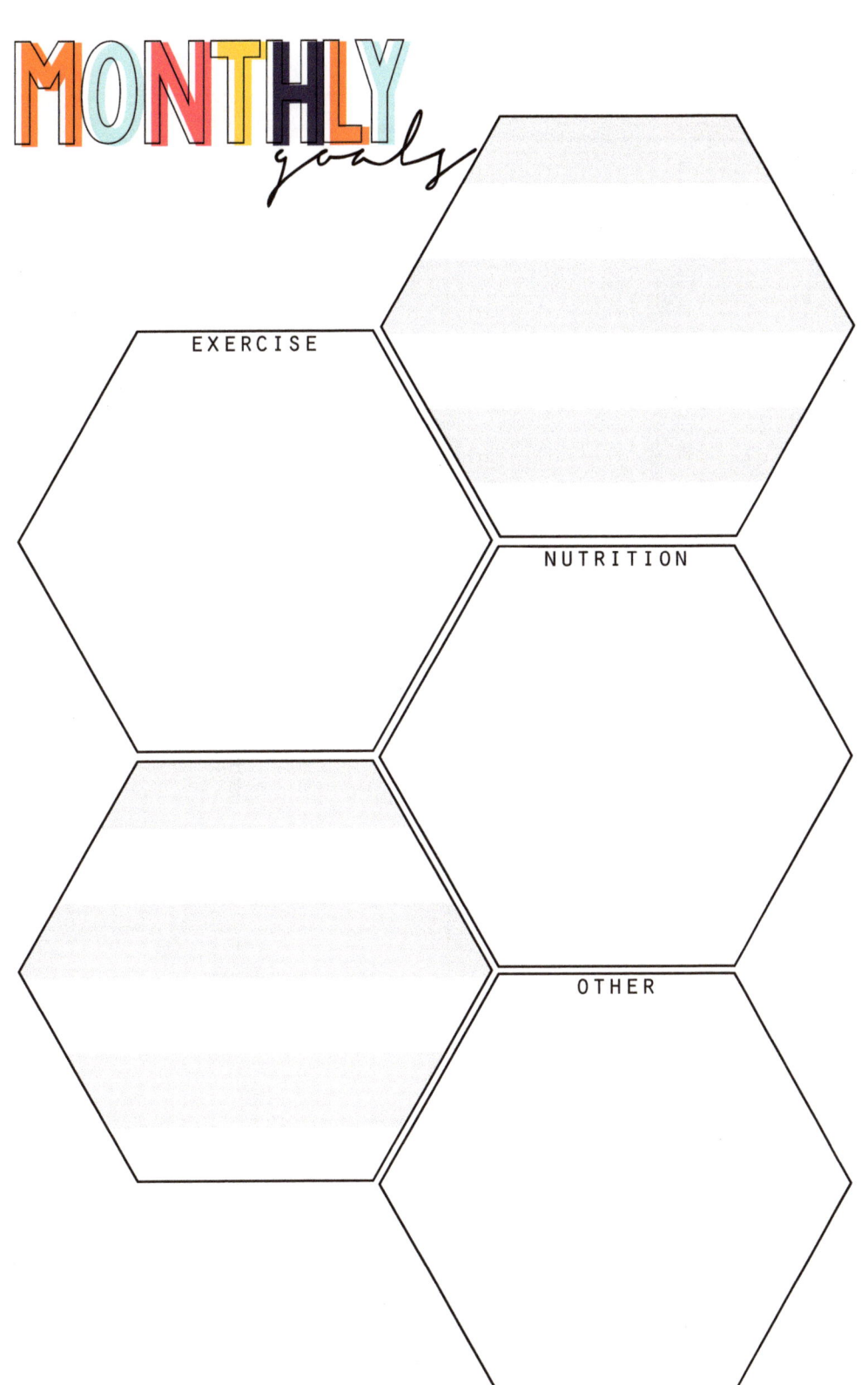

MONTHLY goals

EXERCISE

NUTRITION

OTHER

MONTH one

MONDAY	TUESDAY	WEDNESDAY	THURSDAY

MONTHLY REVIEW		
MEASUREMENT	CURRENT	FINAL
ARMS		
CHEST		
WAIST		
HIPS		
THIGHS		
WEIGHT		

FRIDAY	SATURDAY	SUNDAY

NOTES

SHOPPING *list*

PROTEIN	HEALTHY FATS
○	○ ....
○	○ ....
○	○ ....
○	○ ....
○	○ ....
○	○ ....
○	○ ....
○	○ ....

FRUITS & VEGGIES	OTHER
○	○ ....
○	○ ....
○	○ ....
○	○ ....
○	○ ....
○	○ ....
○	○ ....
○	○ ....

MEAL *plan*

WEEK OF:

MONDAY

TUESDAY

WEDNESDAY

THURSDAY

FRIDAY

SATURDAY

SUNDAY

GOALS
this week

○ ....
○ ....
○ ....
○ ....

WINS
this week

....
....
....
....

WEEK *of*

	MONDAY	TUESDAY	WEDNESDAY
BREAKFAST			
LUNCH			
DINNER			
WORKOUT			
JOURNAL			

THURSDAY	FRIDAY	SATURDAY	SUNDAY

SHOPPING list

PROTEIN	HEALTHY FATS
○	○ ....
○	○ ....
○	○ ....
○	○ ....
○	○ ....
○	○ ....
○	○ ....
○	○ ....

FRUITS & VEGGIES	OTHER
○	○ ....
○	○ ....
○	○ ....
○	○ ....
○	○ ....
○	○ ....
○	○ ....
○	○ ....

MEAL *plan*

WEEK OF:

MONDAY

TUESDAY

WEDNESDAY

THURSDAY

FRIDAY

SATURDAY

SUNDAY

GOALS
this week

○ ....
○ ....
○ ....
○ ....

WINS
this week

....
....
....
....

WEEK *of* _____

	MONDAY	TUESDAY	WEDNESDAY
BREAKFAST			
LUNCH			
DINNER			
WORKOUT			
JOURNAL			

SHOPPING *list*

PROTEIN	HEALTHY FATS
○	○ ....
○	○ ....
○	○ ....
○	○ ....
○	○ ....
○	○ ....
○	○ ....
○	○ ....

FRUITS & VEGGIES	OTHER
○	○ ....
○	○ ....
○	○ ....
○	○ ....
○	○ ....
○	○ ....
○	○ ....
○	○ ....

MEAL *plan*

MONDAY

TUESDAY

WEDNESDAY

THURSDAY

FRIDAY

SATURDAY

SUNDAY

GOALS
this week

○ ....
○ ....
○ ....
○ ....

WINS
this week

....
....
....
....

WEEK of

	MONDAY	TUESDAY	WEDNESDAY
BREAKFAST			
LUNCH			
DINNER			
WORKOUT			
JOURNAL			

THURSDAY	FRIDAY	SATURDAY	SUNDAY

SHOPPING list

PROTEIN	HEALTHY FATS
○	○ ....
○	○ ....
○	○ ....
○	○ ....
○	○ ....
○	○ ....
○	○ ....
○	○ ....

FRUITS & VEGGIES	OTHER
○	○ ....
○	○ ....
○	○ ....
○	○ ....
○	○ ....
○	○ ....
○	○ ....
○	○ ....

MEAL plan

WEEK OF:

MONDAY	
TUESDAY	
WEDNESDAY	
THURSDAY	
FRIDAY	
SATURDAY	
SUNDAY	

GOALS
this week

○ ....

○ ....

○ ....

○ ....

WINS
this week

....

....

....

....

WEEK *of*

	MONDAY	TUESDAY	WEDNESDAY
BREAKFAST			
LUNCH			
DINNER			
	💧💧💧💧💧💧💧	💧💧💧💧💧💧💧	💧💧💧💧💧💧💧
WORKOUT			
JOURNAL			

THURSDAY	FRIDAY	SATURDAY	SUNDAY

SHOPPING list

PROTEIN	HEALTHY FATS
○	○
○	○
○	○
○	○
○	○
○	○
○	○
○	○

FRUITS & VEGGIES	OTHER
○	○
○	○
○	○
○	○
○	○
○	○
○	○
○	○

MEAL *plan*

WEEK OF:

MONDAY

TUESDAY

WEDNESDAY

THURSDAY

FRIDAY

SATURDAY

SUNDAY

GOALS
this week

○ ....
○ ....
○ ....
○ ....

WINS
this week

....
....
....
....

WEEK of

	MONDAY	TUESDAY	WEDNESDAY
BREAKFAST			
LUNCH			
DINNER			
WORKOUT			
JOURNAL			

THURSDAY	FRIDAY	SATURDAY	SUNDAY

ALL YOUR DREAMS

¡ Are possible !

if you have

the courage

TO FIGHT

FOR

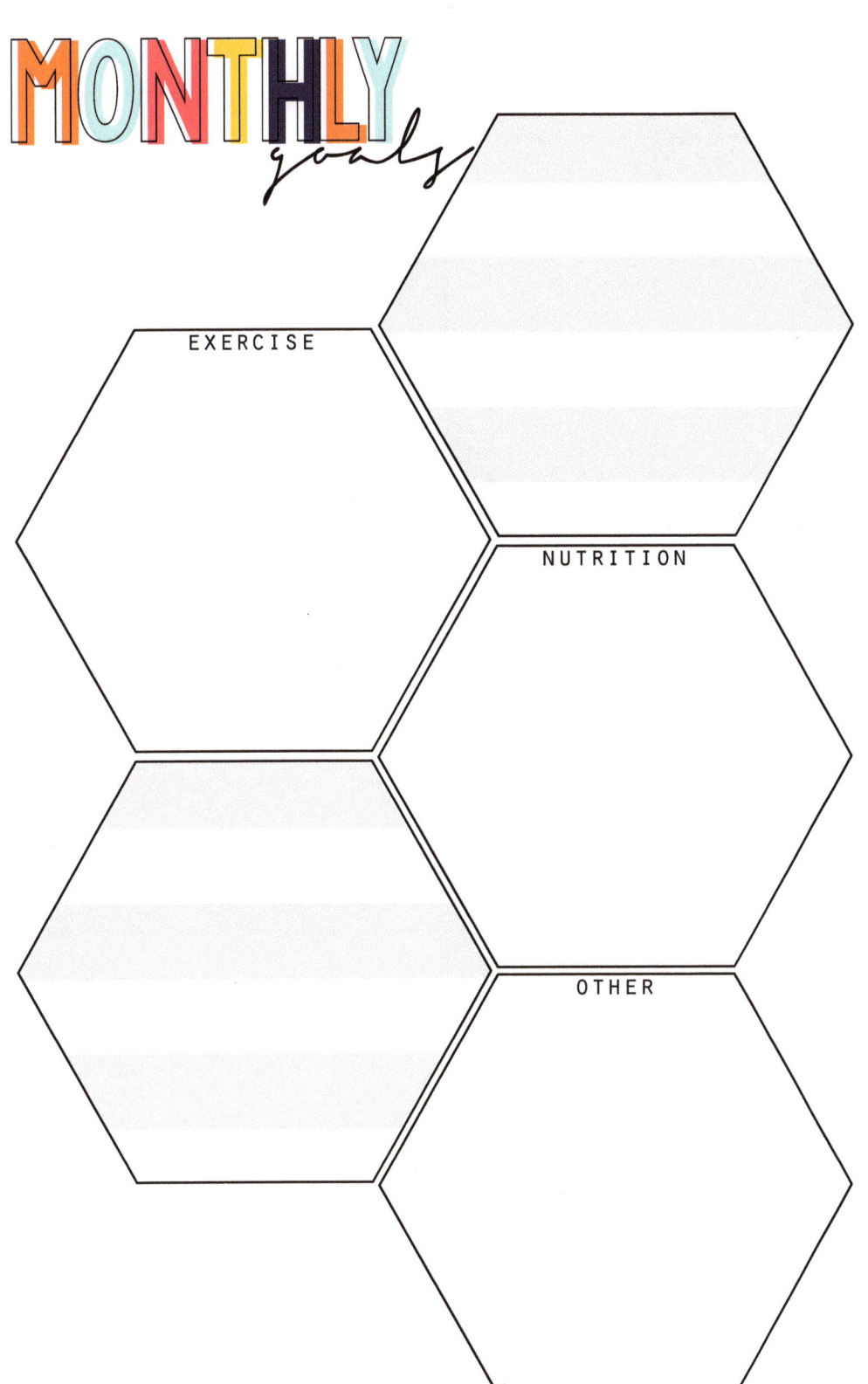

MONTHLY goals

EXERCISE

NUTRITION

OTHER

MONTH two

MONDAY	TUESDAY	WEDNESDAY	THURSDAY

MONTHLY REVIEW

MEASUREMENT	CURRENT	FINAL
ARMS		
CHEST		
WAIST		
HIPS		
THIGHS		
WEIGHT		

FRIDAY	SATURDAY	SUNDAY

NOTES

SHOPPING list

PROTEIN	HEALTHY FATS
○	○ ....
○	○ ....
○	○ ....
○	○ ....
○	○ ....
○	○ ....
○	○ ....
○	○ ....

FRUITS & VEGGIES	OTHER
○	○ ....
○	○ ....
○	○ ....
○	○ ....
○	○ ....
○	○ ....
○	○ ....
○	○ ....

MEAL plan

WEEK OF:

MONDAY	
TUESDAY	
WEDNESDAY	
THURSDAY	
FRIDAY	
SATURDAY	
SUNDAY	

GOALS
this week

- o ....
- o ....
- o ....
- o ....

WINS
this week

....
....
....
....

WEEK of

	MONDAY	TUESDAY	WEDNESDAY
BREAKFAST			
LUNCH			
DINNER			
WORKOUT			
JOURNAL			

THURSDAY	FRIDAY	SATURDAY	SUNDAY

SHOPPING list

PROTEIN	HEALTHY FATS
○	○
○	○
○	○
○	○
○	○
○	○
○	○
○	○

FRUITS & VEGGIES	OTHER
○	○
○	○
○	○
○	○
○	○
○	○
○	○
○	○

MEAL plan

MONDAY

TUESDAY

WEDNESDAY

THURSDAY

FRIDAY

SATURDAY

SUNDAY

GOALS
this week

○ . . . .

○ . . . .

○ . . . .

○ . . . .

WINS
this week

. . . .

. . . .

. . . .

. . . .

WEEK of

	MONDAY	TUESDAY	WEDNESDAY
BREAKFAST			
LUNCH			
DINNER			
WORKOUT			
JOURNAL			

THURSDAY	FRIDAY	SATURDAY	SUNDAY

SHOPPING *list*

PROTEIN	HEALTHY FATS
○	○ ....
○	○ ....
○	○ ....
○	○ ....
○	○ ....
○	○ ....
○	○ ....
○	○ ....

FRUITS & VEGGIES	OTHER
○	○ ....
○	○ ....
○	○ ....
○	○ ....
○	○ ....
○	○ ....
○	○ ....
○	○ ....

MEAL plan

WEEK OF:

MONDAY

TUESDAY

WEDNESDAY

THURSDAY

FRIDAY

SATURDAY

SUNDAY

GOALS
this week

- ○ . . . .
- ○ . . . .
- ○ . . . .
- ○ . . . .

WINS
this week

. . . .

. . . .

. . . .

. . . .

WEEK of

	MONDAY	TUESDAY	WEDNESDAY
BREAKFAST			
LUNCH			
DINNER			
WORKOUT			
JOURNAL			

THURSDAY	FRIDAY	SATURDAY	SUNDAY

SHOPPING list

PROTEIN	HEALTHY FATS
○	○ ....
○	○ ....
○	○ ....
○	○ ....
○	○ ....
○	○ ....
○	○ ....
○	○ ....

FRUITS & VEGGIES	OTHER
○	○ ....
○	○ ....
○	○ ....
○	○ ....
○	○ ....
○	○ ....
○	○ ....
○	○ ....

MEAL plan

WEEK OF:

MONDAY

TUESDAY

WEDNESDAY

THURSDAY

FRIDAY

SATURDAY

SUNDAY

GOALS
this week

- ○ ....
- ○ ....
- ○ ....
- ○ ....

WINS
this week

....
....
....
....

WEEK of

	MONDAY	TUESDAY	WEDNESDAY
BREAKFAST			
LUNCH			
DINNER			
WORKOUT			
JOURNAL			

THURSDAY	FRIDAY	SATURDAY	SUNDAY

SHOPPING list

PROTEIN	HEALTHY FATS
○	○
○	○
○	○
○	○
○	○
○	○
○	○
○	○

FRUITS & VEGGIES	OTHER
○	○
○	○
○	○
○	○
○	○
○	○
○	○
○	○

MEAL *plan*

MONDAY

TUESDAY

WEDNESDAY

THURSDAY

FRIDAY

SATURDAY

SUNDAY

GOALS
this week

○ ....
○ ....
○ ....
○ ....

WINS
this week

....
....
....
....

WEEK *of*

	MONDAY	TUESDAY	WEDNESDAY
BREAKFAST			
LUNCH			
DINNER			
WORKOUT			
JOURNAL			

THURSDAY	FRIDAY	SATURDAY	SUNDAY

DREAM BIG WORK HARD

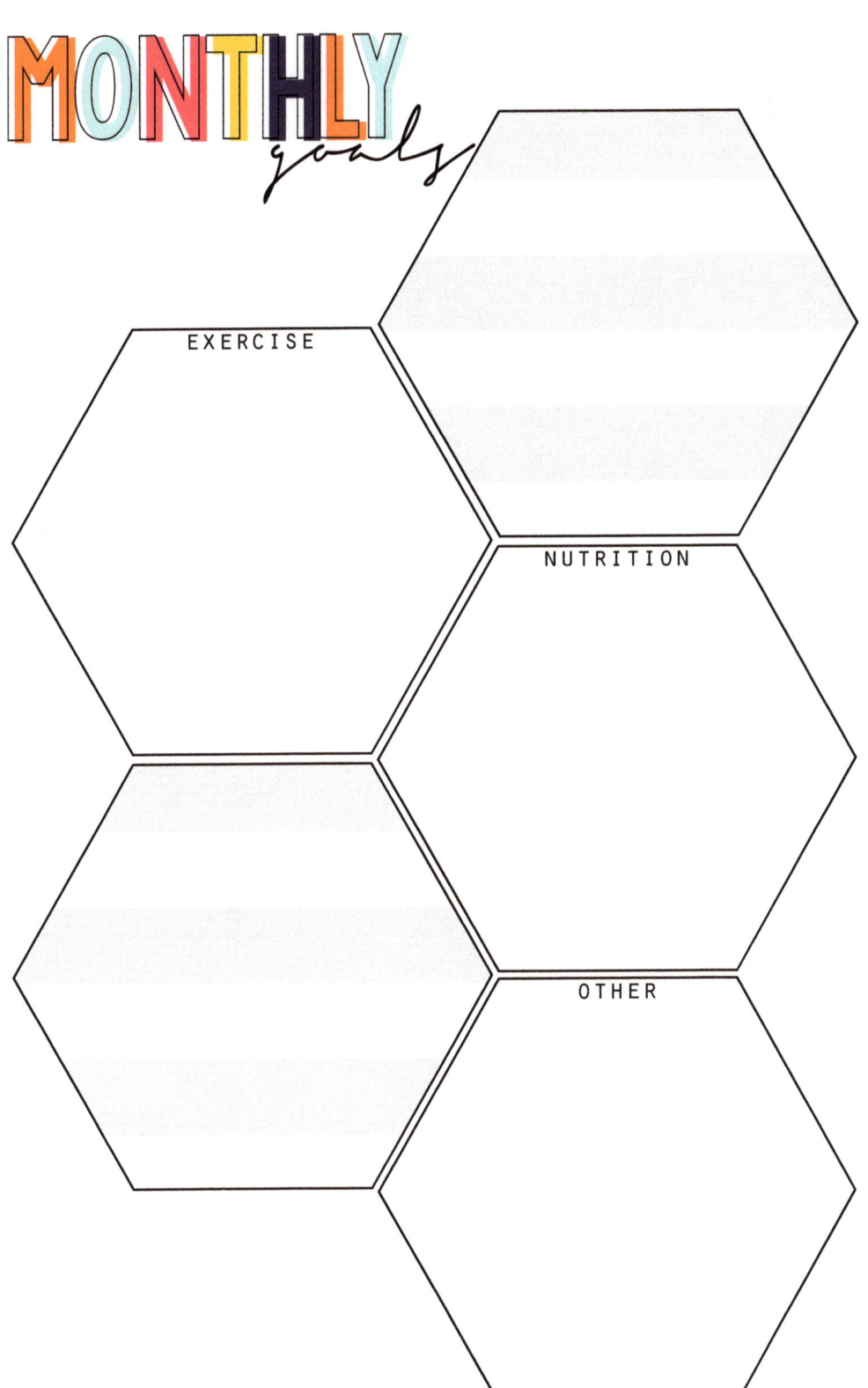

MONTHLY goals

EXERCISE

NUTRITION

OTHER

MONTH

MONDAY	TUESDAY	WEDNESDAY	THURSDAY

MONTHLY REVIEW

MEASUREMENT	CURRENT	FINAL
ARMS		
CHEST		
WAIST		
HIPS		
THIGHS		
WEIGHT		

JAN FEB MAR APR MAY JUN JUL AUG SEP OCT NOV DEC

FRIDAY	SATURDAY	SUNDAY

NOTES

SHOPPING *list*

PROTEIN	HEALTHY FATS
○	○ ....
○	○ ....
○	○ ....
○	○ ....
○	○ ....
○	○ ....
○	○ ....
○	○ ....

FRUITS & VEGGIES	OTHER
○	○ ....
○	○ ....
○	○ ....
○	○ ....
○	○ ....
○	○ ....
○	○ ....
○	○ ....

MEAL *plan*

MONDAY

TUESDAY

WEDNESDAY

THURSDAY

FRIDAY

SATURDAY

SUNDAY

GOALS
this week

- ○ ....
- ○ ....
- ○ ....
- ○ ....

WINS
this week

....
....
....
....

WEEK *of*

	MONDAY	TUESDAY	WEDNESDAY
BREAKFAST			
LUNCH			
DINNER			
WORKOUT			
JOURNAL			

THURSDAY	FRIDAY	SATURDAY	SUNDAY

SHOPPING list

PROTEIN	HEALTHY FATS
○	○
○	○
○	○
○	○
○	○
○	○
○	○
○	○

FRUITS & VEGGIES	OTHER
○	○
○	○
○	○
○	○
○	○
○	○
○	○
○	○

MEAL *plan*

MONDAY

TUESDAY

WEDNESDAY

THURSDAY

FRIDAY

SATURDAY

SUNDAY

GOALS
this week

○ ....
○ ....
○ ....
○ ....

WINS
this week

....
....
....
....

WEEK of

	MONDAY	TUESDAY	WEDNESDAY
BREAKFAST			
LUNCH			
DINNER			
	🌢🌢🌢🌢🌢🌢🌢🌢	🌢🌢🌢🌢🌢🌢🌢🌢	🌢🌢🌢🌢🌢🌢🌢🌢
WORKOUT			
JOURNAL			

THURSDAY	FRIDAY	SATURDAY	SUNDAY

SHOPPING list

PROTEIN	HEALTHY FATS
⭘	⭘
⭘	⭘
⭘	⭘
⭘	⭘
⭘	⭘
⭘	⭘
⭘	⭘
⭘	⭘

FRUITS & VEGGIES	OTHER
⭘	⭘
⭘	⭘
⭘	⭘
⭘	⭘
⭘	⭘
⭘	⭘
⭘	⭘
⭘	⭘

MEAL *plan*

MONDAY

TUESDAY

WEDNESDAY

THURSDAY

FRIDAY

SATURDAY

SUNDAY

GOALS
this week

○ . . . .

○ . . . .

○ . . . .

○ . . . .

WINS
this week

. . . .

. . . .

. . . .

. . . .

WEEK *of*

	MONDAY	TUESDAY	WEDNESDAY
BREAKFAST			
LUNCH			
DINNER			
WORKOUT			
JOURNAL			

THURSDAY	FRIDAY	SATURDAY	SUNDAY

SHOPPING list

PROTEIN	HEALTHY FATS
○	○ ....
○	○ ....
○	○ ....
○	○ ....
○	○ ....
○	○ ....
○	○ ....
○	○ ....

FRUITS & VEGGIES	OTHER
○	○ ....
○	○ ....
○	○ ....
○	○ ....
○	○ ....
○	○ ....
○	○ ....
○	○ ....

MEAL *plan*

WEEK OF:

MONDAY

TUESDAY

WEDNESDAY

THURSDAY

FRIDAY

SATURDAY

SUNDAY

GOALS
this week

○ ....
○ ....
○ ....
○ ....

WINS
this week

....
....
....
....

WEEK of

	MONDAY	TUESDAY	WEDNESDAY
BREAKFAST			
LUNCH			
DINNER			
	💧💧💧💧💧💧💧	💧💧💧💧💧💧	💧💧💧💧💧💧
WORKOUT			
JOURNAL			

THURSDAY	FRIDAY	SATURDAY	SUNDAY

SHOPPING *list*

PROTEIN	HEALTHY FATS
○	○ ....
○	○ ....
○	○ ....
○	○ ....
○	○ ....
○	○ ....
○	○ ....
○	○ ....

FRUITS & VEGGIES	OTHER
○	○ ....
○	○ ....
○	○ ....
○	○ ....
○	○ ....
○	○ ....
○	○ ....
○	○ ....

MEAL *plan*

WEEK OF:

MONDAY

TUESDAY

WEDNESDAY

THURSDAY

FRIDAY

SATURDAY

SUNDAY

GOALS
this week

○ ....
○ ....
○ ....
○ ....

WINS
this week

....
....
....
....

WEEK *of*

	MONDAY	TUESDAY	WEDNESDAY
BREAKFAST			
LUNCH			
DINNER			
WORKOUT			
JOURNAL			

THURSDAY	FRIDAY	SATURDAY	SUNDAY

Be

WHO
YOU ARE

IN ALL THE

Beautiful

little
WAYS

you can

think of.

MONTHLY *goals*

EXERCISE

NUTRITION

OTHER

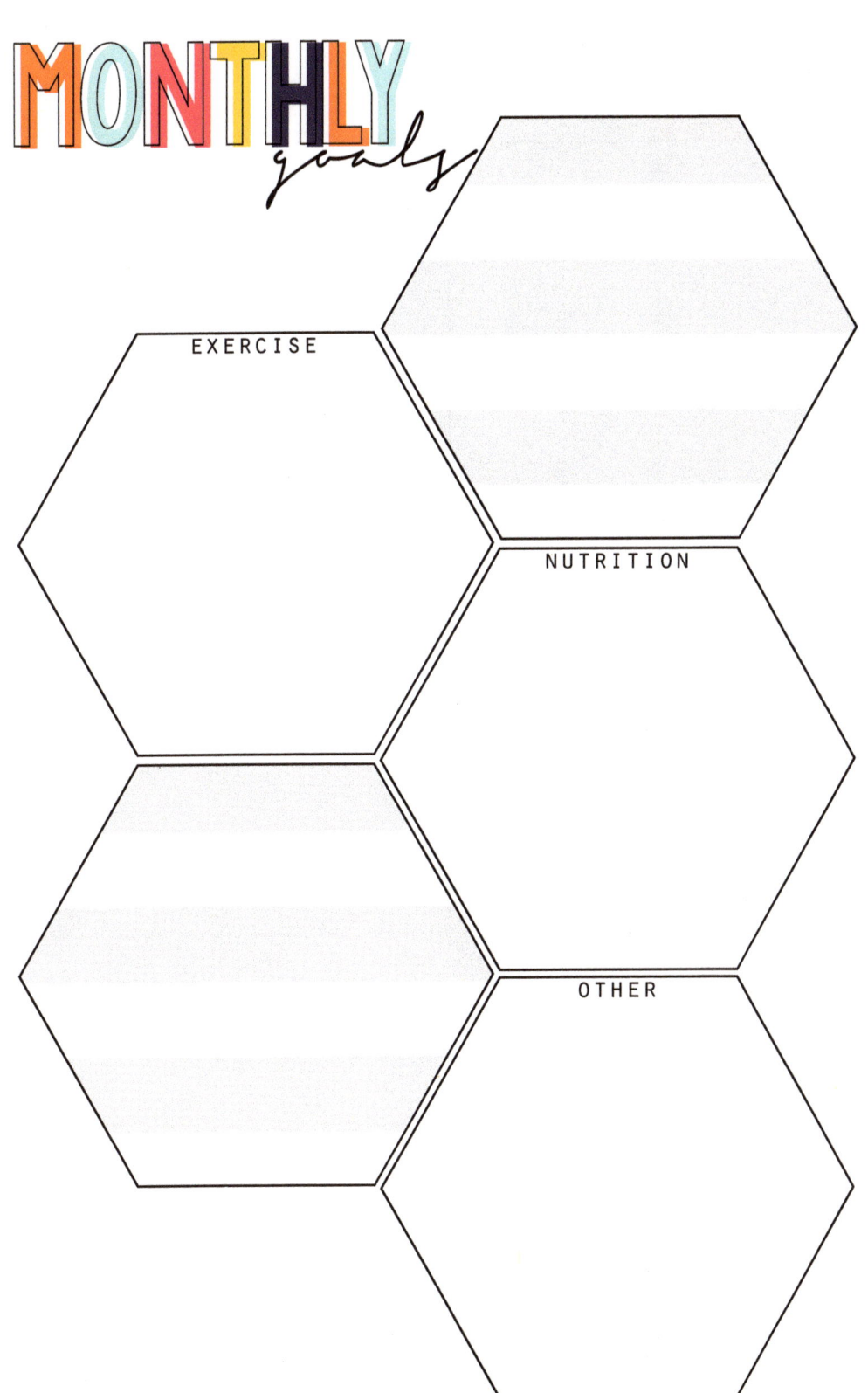

MONTH *four*

MONDAY	TUESDAY	WEDNESDAY	THURSDAY

MONTHLY REVIEW		
MEASUREMENT	CURRENT	FINAL
ARMS		
CHEST		
WAIST		
HIPS		
THIGHS		
WEIGHT		

FRIDAY	SATURDAY	SUNDAY

NOTES

SHOPPING list

PROTEIN	HEALTHY FATS
○	○
○	○
○	○
○	○
○	○
○	○
○	○
○	○

FRUITS & VEGGIES	OTHER
○	○
○	○
○	○
○	○
○	○
○	○
○	○
○	○

MEAL plan

WEEK OF:

MONDAY

TUESDAY

WEDNESDAY

THURSDAY

FRIDAY

SATURDAY

SUNDAY

GOALS
this week

○ ....
○ ....
○ ....
○ ....

WINS
this week

....
....
....
....

WEEK *of* ____

	MONDAY	TUESDAY	WEDNESDAY
BREAKFAST			
LUNCH			
DINNER			
WORKOUT			
JOURNAL			

THURSDAY	FRIDAY	SATURDAY	SUNDAY

SHOPPING list

PROTEIN	HEALTHY FATS
○	○ ....
○	○ ....
○	○ ....
○	○ ....
○	○ ....
○	○ ....
○	○ ....
○	○ ....

FRUITS & VEGGIES	OTHER
○	○ ....
○	○ ....
○	○ ....
○	○ ....
○	○ ....
○	○ ....
○	○ ....
○	○ ....

MEAL plan

WEEK OF:

MONDAY

TUESDAY

WEDNESDAY

THURSDAY

FRIDAY

SATURDAY

SUNDAY

GOALS
this week

- ○ ....
- ○ ....
- ○ ....
- ○ ....

WINS
this week

....
....
....
....

WEEK *of*

	MONDAY	TUESDAY	WEDNESDAY
BREAKFAST			
LUNCH			
DINNER			
WORKOUT			
JOURNAL			

THURSDAY	FRIDAY	SATURDAY	SUNDAY

SHOPPING list

PROTEIN	HEALTHY FATS
○	○ ....
○	○ ....
○	○ ....
○	○ ....
○	○ ....
○	○ ....
○	○ ....
○	○ ....

FRUITS & VEGGIES	OTHER
○	○ ....
○	○ ....
○	○ ....
○	○ ....
○	○ ....
○	○ ....
○	○ ....
○	○ ....

MEAL *plan*

WEEK OF:

MONDAY

TUESDAY

WEDNESDAY

THURSDAY

FRIDAY

SATURDAY

SUNDAY

GOALS
this week

○ ....
○ ....
○ ....
○ ....

WINS
this week

....
....
....
....

WEEK *of*

	MONDAY	TUESDAY	WEDNESDAY
BREAKFAST			
LUNCH			
DINNER			
	💧💧💧💧💧💧💧💧	💧💧💧💧💧💧💧💧	💧💧💧💧💧💧💧💧
WORKOUT			
JOURNAL			

THURSDAY	FRIDAY	SATURDAY	SUNDAY

SHOPPING list

PROTEIN	HEALTHY FATS
○	○
○	○
○	○
○	○
○	○
○	○
○	○
○	○

FRUITS & VEGGIES	OTHER
○	○
○	○
○	○
○	○
○	○
○	○
○	○
○	○

MEAL *plan*

WEEK OF:

MONDAY

TUESDAY

WEDNESDAY

THURSDAY

FRIDAY

SATURDAY

SUNDAY

GOALS
this week

○ ....
○ ....
○ ....
○ ....

WINS
this week

....
....
....
....

WEEK of

	MONDAY	TUESDAY	WEDNESDAY
BREAKFAST			
LUNCH			
DINNER			
WORKOUT			
JOURNAL			

THURSDAY	FRIDAY	SATURDAY	SUNDAY

SHOPPING list

PROTEIN	HEALTHY FATS
○	○ ....
○	○ ....
○	○ ....
○	○ ....
○	○ ....
○	○ ....
○	○ ....
○	○ ....

FRUITS & VEGGIES	OTHER
○	○ ....
○	○ ....
○	○ ....
○	○ ....
○	○ ....
○	○ ....
○	○ ....
○	○ ....

MEAL *plan*

WEEK OF:

MONDAY

TUESDAY

WEDNESDAY

THURSDAY

FRIDAY

SATURDAY

SUNDAY

○ ....
○ ....
○ ....
○ ....

WINS *this week*

....
....
....
....

WEEK *of* _____

	MONDAY	TUESDAY	WEDNESDAY
BREAKFAST			
LUNCH			
DINNER			
WORKOUT			
JOURNAL			

THURSDAY	FRIDAY	SATURDAY	SUNDAY

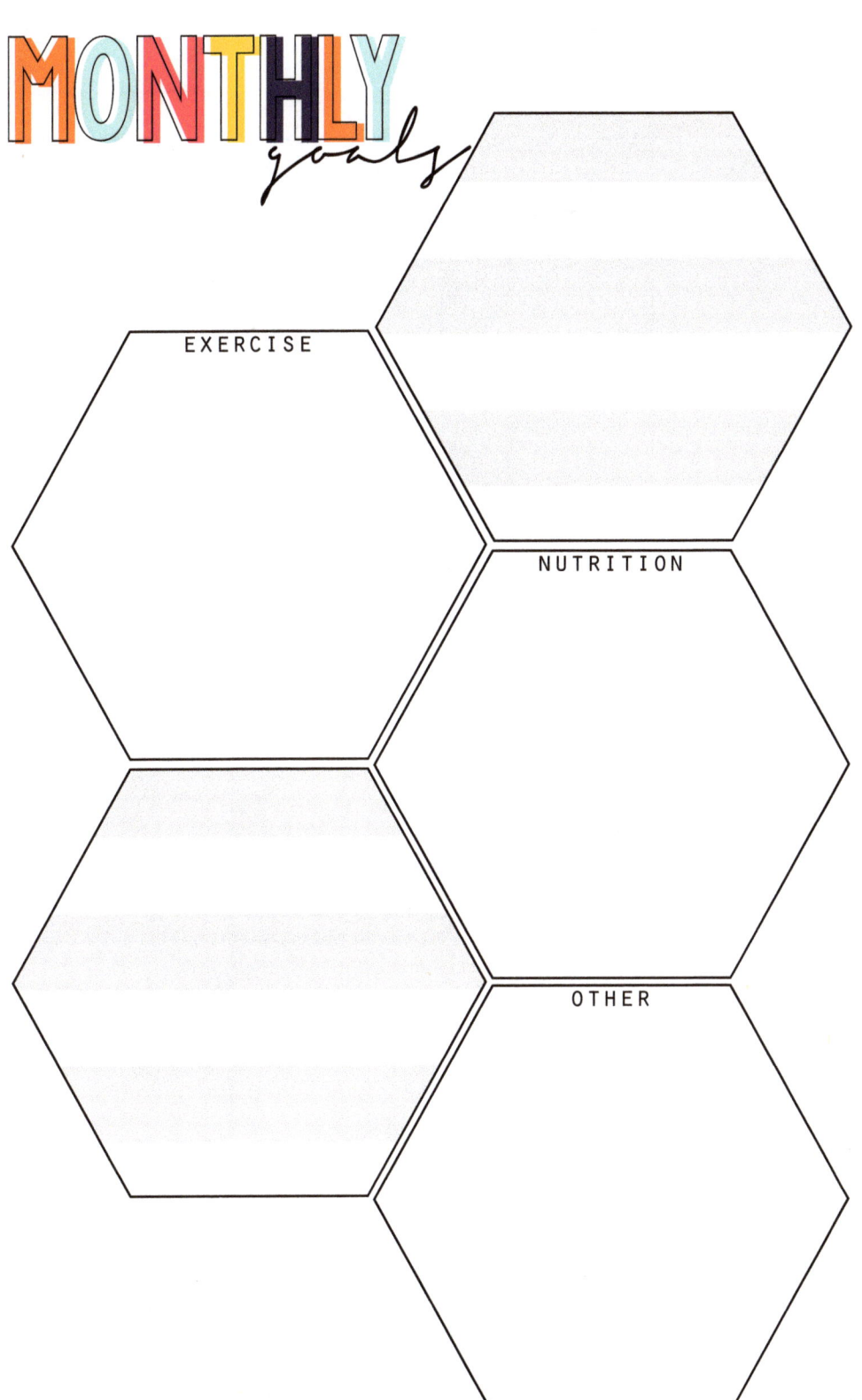

MONTHLY goals

EXERCISE

NUTRITION

OTHER

MONTH *five*

MONDAY	TUESDAY	WEDNESDAY	THURSDAY

MONTHLY REVIEW

MEASUREMENT	CURRENT	FINAL
ARMS		
CHEST		
WAIST		
HIPS		
THIGHS		
WEIGHT		

JAN FEB MAR APR MAY JUN JUL AUG SEP OCT NOV DEC

FRIDAY	SATURDAY	SUNDAY

NOTES

SHOPPING list

PROTEIN	HEALTHY FATS
○	○ ....
○	○ ....
○	○ ....
○	○ ....
○	○ ....
○	○ ....
○	○ ....
○	○ ....

FRUITS & VEGGIES	OTHER
○	○ ....
○	○ ....
○	○ ....
○	○ ....
○	○ ....
○	○ ....
○	○ ....
○	○ ....

MEAL plan

WEEK OF:

MONDAY

TUESDAY

WEDNESDAY

THURSDAY

FRIDAY

SATURDAY

SUNDAY

GOALS
this week

○ ....

○ ....

○ ....

○ ....

WINS
this week

....

....

....

....

WEEK of

	MONDAY	TUESDAY	WEDNESDAY
BREAKFAST			
LUNCH			
DINNER			
WORKOUT			
JOURNAL			

THURSDAY	FRIDAY	SATURDAY	SUNDAY

SHOPPING *list*

PROTEIN	HEALTHY FATS
○	○
○	○
○	○
○	○
○	○
○	○
○	○
○	○

FRUITS & VEGGIES	OTHER
○	○
○	○
○	○
○	○
○	○
○	○
○	○
○	○

MEAL plan

MONDAY

TUESDAY

WEDNESDAY

THURSDAY

FRIDAY

SATURDAY

SUNDAY

GOALS
this week

- O ....
- O ....
- O ....
- O ....

WINS
this week

....

....

....

....

WEEK *of* _____

	MONDAY	TUESDAY	WEDNESDAY
BREAKFAST			
LUNCH			
DINNER			
WORKOUT			
JOURNAL			

THURSDAY	FRIDAY	SATURDAY	SUNDAY

SHOPPING list

PROTEIN	HEALTHY FATS
○	○
○	○
○	○
○	○
○	○
○	○
○	○
○	○

FRUITS & VEGGIES	OTHER
○	○
○	○
○	○
○	○
○	○
○	○
○	○
○	○

MEAL plan

WEEK OF:

MONDAY

TUESDAY

WEDNESDAY

THURSDAY

FRIDAY

SATURDAY

SUNDAY

GOALS
this week

○ ....
○ ....
○ ....
○ ....

WINS
this week

....
....
....
....

WEEK *of*

	MONDAY	TUESDAY	WEDNESDAY
BREAKFAST			
LUNCH			
DINNER			
	💧💧💧💧💧💧💧	💧💧💧💧💧💧💧	💧💧💧💧💧💧💧
WORKOUT			
JOURNAL			

THURSDAY	FRIDAY	SATURDAY	SUNDAY

SHOPPING list

PROTEIN	HEALTHY FATS
○	○
○	○
○	○
○	○
○	○
○	○
○	○
○	○

FRUITS & VEGGIES	OTHER
○	○
○	○
○	○
○	○
○	○
○	○
○	○
○	○

MEAL plan

WEEK OF:

MONDAY

TUESDAY

WEDNESDAY

THURSDAY

FRIDAY

SATURDAY

SUNDAY

GOALS
this week

○ ....
○ ....
○ ....
○ ....

WINS
this week

....
....
....
....

WEEK *of* _____

	MONDAY	TUESDAY	WEDNESDAY
BREAKFAST			
LUNCH			
DINNER			
WORKOUT			
JOURNAL			

THURSDAY	FRIDAY	SATURDAY	SUNDAY

SHOPPING list

PROTEIN	HEALTHY FATS
○	○
○	○
○	○
○	○
○	○
○	○
○	○
○	○

FRUITS & VEGGIES	OTHER
○	○
○	○
○	○
○	○
○	○
○	○
○	○
○	○

MEAL *plan*

WEEK OF:

MONDAY

TUESDAY

WEDNESDAY

THURSDAY

FRIDAY

SATURDAY

SUNDAY

GOALS
this week

- O ....
- O ....
- O ....
- O ....

WINS
this week

....
....
....
....

WEEK of

	MONDAY	TUESDAY	WEDNESDAY
BREAKFAST			
LUNCH			
DINNER			
WORKOUT			
JOURNAL			

THURSDAY	FRIDAY	SATURDAY	SUNDAY

if it doesn't
challenge
you
it doesn't
change
you

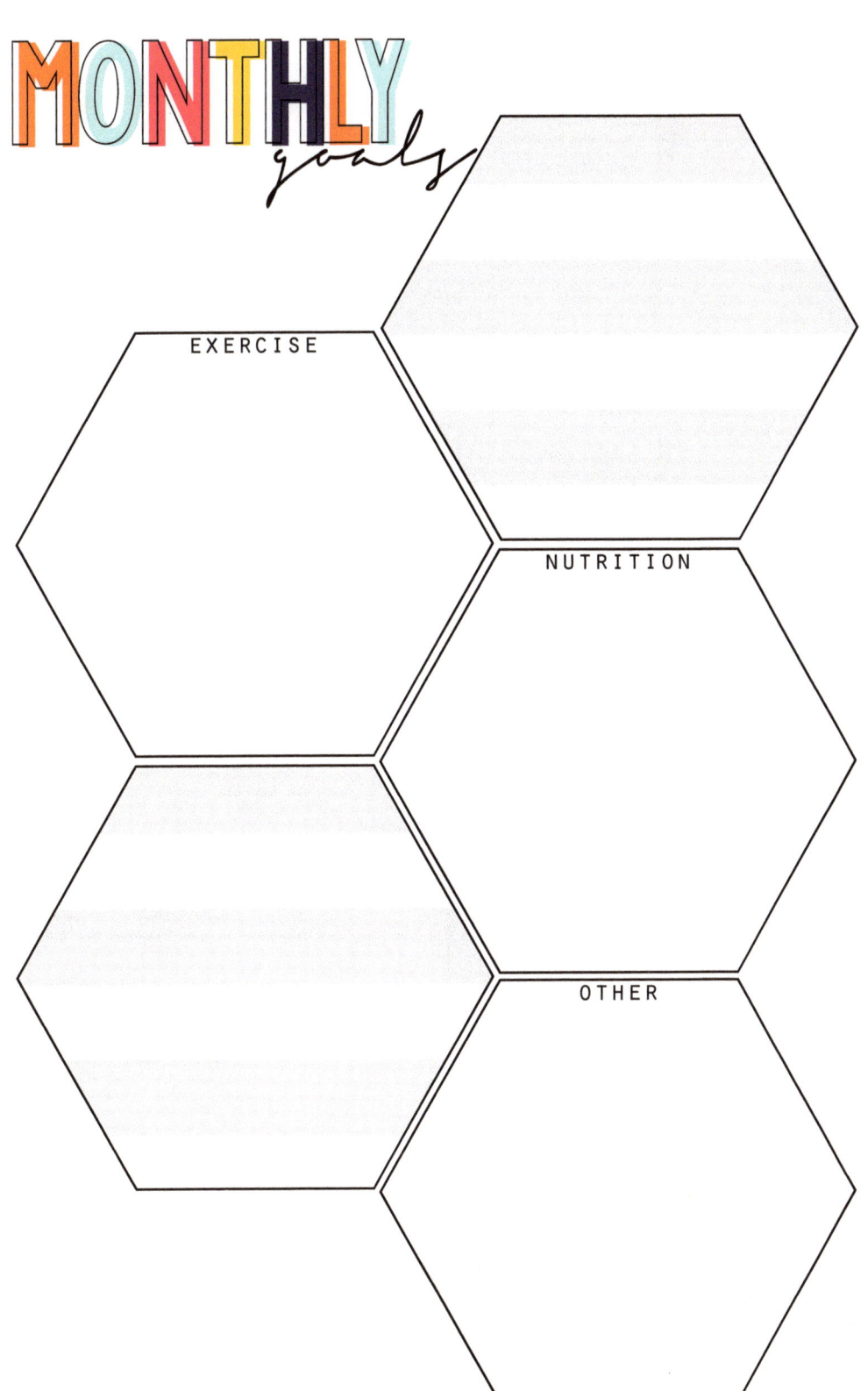

MONTHLY goals

EXERCISE

NUTRITION

OTHER

MONTH *six*

MONDAY	TUESDAY	WEDNESDAY	THURSDAY

MONTHLY REVIEW		
MEASUREMENT	CURRENT	FINAL
ARMS		
CHEST		
WAIST		
HIPS		
THIGHS		
WEIGHT		

FRIDAY	SATURDAY	SUNDAY

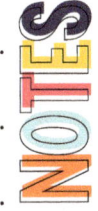

SHOPPING list

PROTEIN	HEALTHY FATS
○	○ ....
○	○ ....
○	○ ....
○	○ ....
○	○ ....
○	○ ....
○	○ ....
○	○ ....

FRUITS & VEGGIES	OTHER
○	○ ....
○	○ ....
○	○ ....
○	○ ....
○	○ ....
○	○ ....
○	○ ....
○	○ ....

MEAL plan

WEEK OF:

MONDAY	
TUESDAY	
WEDNESDAY	
THURSDAY	
FRIDAY	
SATURDAY	
SUNDAY	

GOALS
this week

○ ....

○ ....

○ ....

○ ....

WINS
this week

....

....

....

....

WEEK of

	MONDAY	TUESDAY	WEDNESDAY
BREAKFAST			
LUNCH			
DINNER			
WORKOUT			
JOURNAL			

THURSDAY	FRIDAY	SATURDAY	SUNDAY

SHOPPING list

PROTEIN	HEALTHY FATS
○	○
○	○
○	○
○	○
○	○
○	○
○	○
○	○

FRUITS & VEGGIES	OTHER
○	○
○	○
○	○
○	○
○	○
○	○
○	○
○	○

MEAL *plan*

WEEK OF:

MONDAY

TUESDAY

WEDNESDAY

THURSDAY

FRIDAY

SATURDAY

SUNDAY

GOALS
this week

○ ....

○ ....

○ ....

○ ....

WINS
this week

....

....

....

....

WEEK of

	MONDAY	TUESDAY	WEDNESDAY
BREAKFAST			
LUNCH			
DINNER			
WORKOUT			
JOURNAL			

THURSDAY	FRIDAY	SATURDAY	SUNDAY

SHOPPING list

PROTEIN	HEALTHY FATS
○	○
○	○
○	○
○	○
○	○
○	○
○	○
○	○

FRUITS & VEGGIES	OTHER
○	○
○	○
○	○
○	○
○	○
○	○
○	○
○	○

MEAL *plan*

WEEK OF:

MONDAY

TUESDAY

WEDNESDAY

THURSDAY

FRIDAY

SATURDAY

SUNDAY

GOALS
this week

○ ....

○ ....

○ ....

○ ....

WINS
this week

....

....

....

....

WEEK of

	MONDAY	TUESDAY	WEDNESDAY
BREAKFAST			
LUNCH			
DINNER			
	💧💧💧💧💧💧💧	💧💧💧💧💧💧💧	💧💧💧💧💧💧💧
WORKOUT			
JOURNAL			

THURSDAY	FRIDAY	SATURDAY	SUNDAY

SHOPPING *list*

PROTEIN	HEALTHY FATS
○	○
○	○
○	○
○	○
○	○
○	○
○	○
○	○

FRUITS & VEGGIES	OTHER
○	○
○	○
○	○
○	○
○	○
○	○
○	○
○	○

MEAL *plan*

WEEK OF:

MONDAY

TUESDAY

WEDNESDAY

THURSDAY

FRIDAY

SATURDAY

SUNDAY

GOALS
this week

○ ....
○ ....
○ ....
○ ....

WINS
this week

....
....
....
....

WEEK of

	MONDAY	TUESDAY	WEDNESDAY
BREAKFAST			
LUNCH			
DINNER			
WORKOUT			
JOURNAL			

THURSDAY	FRIDAY	SATURDAY	SUNDAY

SHOPPING list

PROTEIN	HEALTHY FATS
○	○
○	○
○	○
○	○
○	○
○	○
○	○
○	○

FRUITS & VEGGIES	OTHER
○	○
○	○
○	○
○	○
○	○
○	○
○	○
○	○

MEAL plan

MONDAY

TUESDAY

WEDNESDAY

THURSDAY

FRIDAY

SATURDAY

SUNDAY

GOALS
this week

- ○ ....
- ○ ....
- ○ ....
- ○ ....

WINS
this week

....
....
....
....

WEEK of

	MONDAY	TUESDAY	WEDNESDAY
BREAKFAST			
LUNCH			
DINNER			
	〰〰〰〰〰〰	〰〰〰〰〰〰	〰〰〰〰〰〰
WORKOUT			
JOURNAL			

THURSDAY	FRIDAY	SATURDAY	SUNDAY

Lightning Source UK Ltd.
Milton Keynes UK
UKHW020827290519
343469UK00008B/111/P